The Barking Lot
Bird Coloring Book for Kids

The Barking Lot
Bird Coloring Book for Kids

KF Wheatie & KM Wheatie

Strawberryhead &
Gingerbread Press

www.strawberryheadandgingerbread.com

The Barking Lot Bird Coloring Book for Kids

Published by Strawberryhead and Gingerbread Press
https://www.strawberryheadandgingerbread.com

Copyright © 2024 by KF Wheatie & KM Wheatie

All rights reserved. Neither this book, nor any parts within it may be sold or reproduced in any form or by any electronic or mechanical means, including information storage and retrieval systems, without permission in writing from the author. The only exception is by a reviewer, who may quote short excerpts in a review.

ISBN: 979-8-9906129-4-5 (paperback)

Sparrow

Sparrows are small, brown birds that love to chirp and live in groups. They can remember where they've hidden their food, like tiny treasure hunters.

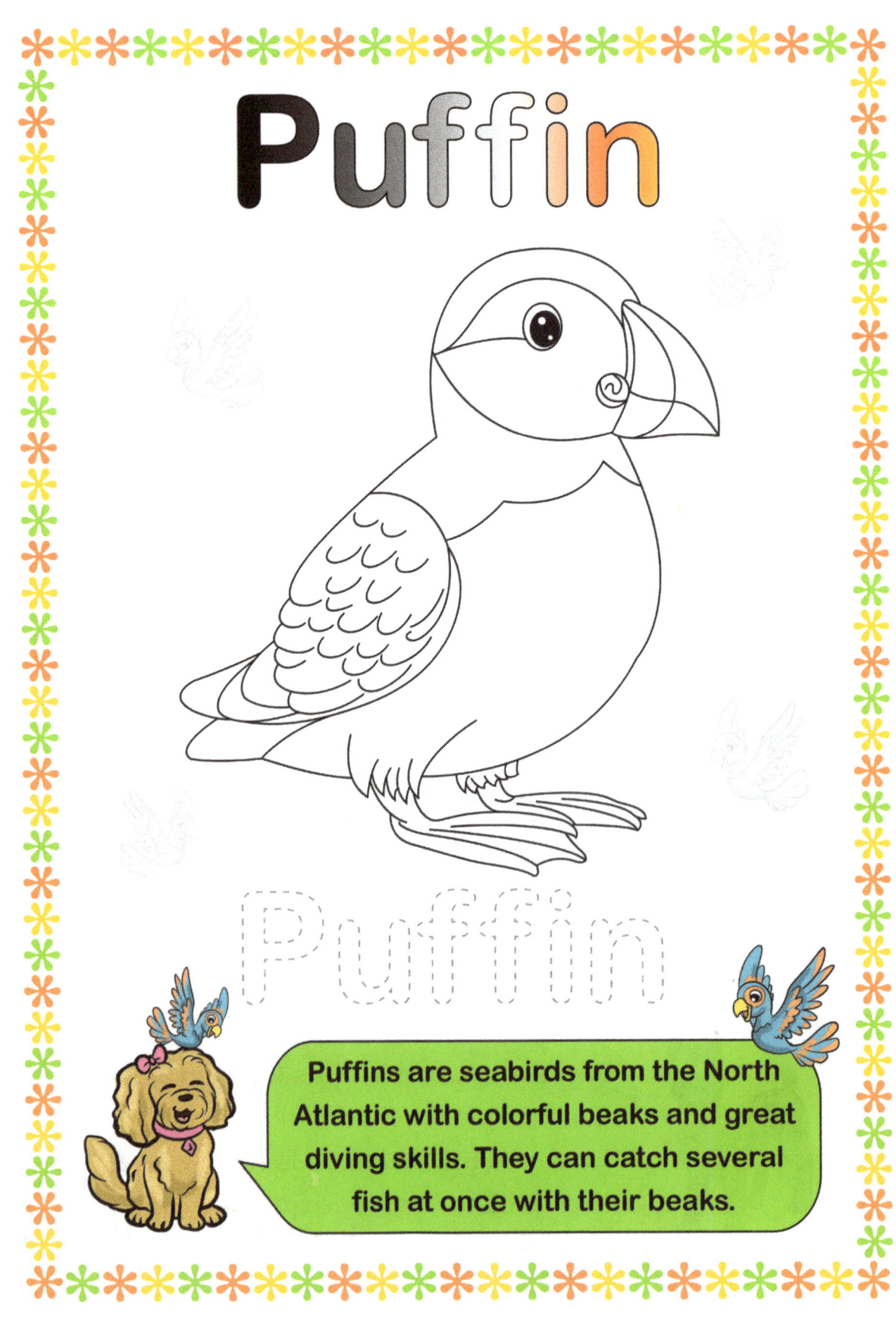

Puffin

Puffins are seabirds from the North Atlantic with colorful beaks and great diving skills. They can catch several fish at once with their beaks.

Woodpecker

Woodpecker

Woodpeckers are birds found in forests that use their strong beaks to drum on trees and create nests. They can peck up to 20 times per second.

Hummingbird

Hummingbird

> Hummingbirds are tiny birds known for their rapid wing beats and ability to hover in place. They feed on nectar from flowers with their long, slender beaks.

Pelican

Pelicans are large water birds known for their long beaks and expandable pouches used to catch fish. They are often seen gliding low over water.

Crow

Crows are intelligent, black birds found in many parts of the world. They are known for their problem-solving skills and complex social behaviors.

Seagull

Seagull

Seagulls are coastal birds known for their white and gray plumage and loud calls. They are skilled at scavenging & often seen near beaches and water.

Hoopoe

Hoopoe

The hoopoe is a colorful bird with a distinctive crest and striking patterns. It is known for its unique "trumpet-like" call and for feeding on insects.

Toucan

Toucans are vibrant, tropical birds known for their large, colorful beaks. They use their beaks to reach and eat fruit high in the trees.

Cockatoo

Cockatoos are intelligent, colorful parrots with distinctive crests on their heads. They are known for their playful behavior and strong social bonds.

Crane

Cranes are tall, elegant birds found in wetlands and grasslands. They are known for their long legs and graceful dancing displays during courtship.

Quails

Quails are small, round birds that like to hide in tall grass. They make soft, cheerful sounds and are great at blending into their surroundings.

Pigeon

Pigeon

Pigeons are common birds with gray feathers and a gentle cooing sound. They can find their way back to their nests from far away.

Swan

Swan

Swans are large, elegant birds with long necks and white feathers. They glide gracefully on water and are known for their beauty.

Owl

Owls are nocturnal birds with large eyes and silent flight. They are known for their wise appearance and ability to see in the dark.

Rooster

Roosters are known for their bright feathers and loud crowing. They use their calls to mark their territory and communicate with other chickens.

Kingfisher

Kingfishers are bright, colorful birds with sharp beaks used to catch fish. They are known for their spectacular dives into water to catch their prey.

Guinea fowl

Guinea fowl

Guineafowl are spotted, ground-dwelling birds known for their unique feather patterns. They are excellent foragers and help control insect populations.

www.ingramcontent.com/pod-product-compliance
Lightning Source LLC
Chambersburg PA
CBHW080535030426
42337CB00023B/4752